Noteworthy
Sermon Notes

By Josh Hamon
Published by The Ministry of War

First Printing: 2019
ISBN 978-1-7339650-9-5
Published by The Ministry of War
Bremerton, WA 98310
TheMinistryofWar.com

Ordering Information:
Special discounts are available on quantity purchases by corporations, associations, educators and others. For details, contact the publisher at the above-listed address or email hello@TheMinistryofWar.com.

U.S. trade bookstores and wholesalers:
Please contact hello@TheMinistryofWar.com.

For my son

Taking Notes: a Mini-Guide

Please use the following pages in any manner that works for you. Here are some of thoughts and tips on outlining. Maybe you are already used to outlining and taking notes in class. However, the sermon is different, and should be treated so. In class you, need notes to study for a test, sermon notes have a few different uses:

- Focus — The act of taking notes, regardless of style, helps you pay attention during the sermon.
- Retention — You may type faster than you write, but what you write is remembered more than what you type.
- Future Reference — With a little organization, your notes are yours forever, seeing what you learned or prayed about in the past.

Notice test prep wasn't on the list? Since that's not a goal, don't worry about capturing everything. Stay focused.

Is the same word being repeated a lot? Write it down.

Did you just hear a word or idea that's new or unfamiliar? Write it down and check it out later.

Let's get tactical:

You'll see that the pages in this book are set up like graph paper. The grid is 35 across and 50 tall. This way, you can write as big or small as needed. You can create your own columns or boxes to organize your notes. Use the grid for writing, sketching or whatever else comes to mind. If you need something to be to scale, remember the grid size. For instance, if you are creating a time-line, remember there are 35 squares across the page. The goal is to give you the flexibility to actively listen.

The headers do have suggestion labels, use them as needed. DO NOT constrain note-taking to one page per sermon. If you enjoy starting a new sermon on a new sheet, go for it, but if you need one more line of notes on a page to complete your notes, do it! This is about note taking, not seeing clean sheets of paper.

Also, here are a few sermon-specific tips based on various sermon styles:

- Pastor asks a question, then proceeds to answer it. Write down the question and the answer.
- Some pastors love numbers, "This text has 4 applications for your life." The sermon is probably divided into 4 sections.
- Some preachers like alliteration (starting many words with the same letter) and that can help you follow along and see the transitions.
- When God, the text or the pastor is speaking to you, write it down, underline it and come back to it later.
- Remember the sermon is part of worship. This is not a speed-writing contest, a spelling contest and you only need enough penmanship (or penteenship) to be legible to you.

How to Take Notes:

1. Create an outline as you go. Outlines are a way to organize notes. They capture key ideas and quotes without using every word.
   A. There is a very good chance the person speaking created an outline for their sermon. Over time you'll learn to "see" it.
   B. When an idea is related to a key idea, use indenting (blank space at the beginning of the line) to show they are connected.
   C. That's what I'm doing here with the main section "How to Take Notes." When I'm done I'll move on to idea number two.
   D. When outlining, if you misspell a word but can still read it, don't bother correcting it, just move on.
      1. But if you need to correct something, don't erase it, ~~kroz~~ cross it out and keep going!
   E. If you don't catch everything, don't worry!
   F. Abbreviate words.
      1. w/ for with
      2. + for and
      3. JC for Jesus
      4. Meth. for Methuselah
      5. Text message abbreviations work great here
      6. Develop your own, these are your notes! Personally, I use vf for verify.
2. Not a fast or legible writer? Draw pictures!
   A. Mind mapping combines words and bubbles to show key ideas.

1. For example:

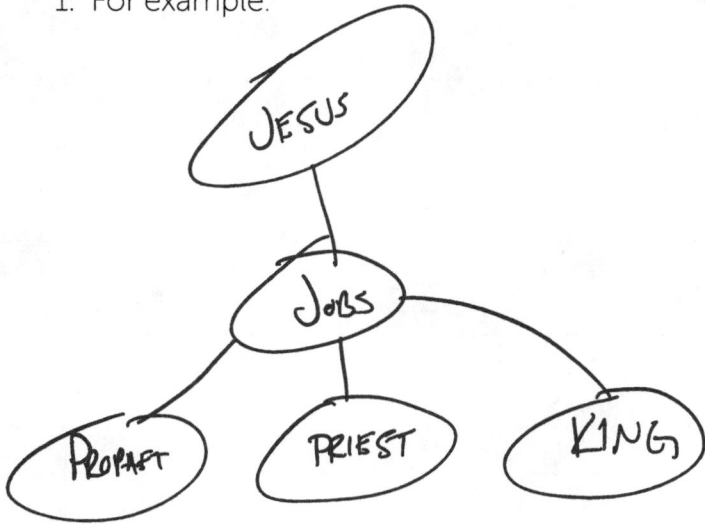

B. Maybe a few, simple comic book panels will help you stay focused.

   1. Create a work of art later. For now, sketch.
   2. Can't draw? Who cares?
   3. For example:

Verses / Title / Topic:
Date:
Other:

Verses / Title / Topic:
Date:
Other:

Verses / Title / Topic:
Date:
Other:

Verses / Title / Topic:
Date:
Other:

4

Verses / Title / Topic:
Date:
Other:

Verses / Title / Topic:
Date:
Other:

Verses / Title / Topic:
Date:
Other:

Verses / Title / Topic:
Date:
Other:

Verses / Title / Topic:
Date:
Other:

Verses / Title / Topic:
Date:
Other:

Verses / Title / Topic:
Date:
Other:

Verses / Title / Topic:
Date:
Other:

12

Verses / Title / Topic:
Date:
Other:

Verses / Title / Topic:
Date:
Other:

Verses / Title / Topic:
Date:
Other:

Verses / Title / Topic:
Date:
Other:

Verses / Title / Topic:
Date:
Other:

Verses / Title / Topic:
Date:
Other:

Verses / Title / Topic:
Date:
Other:

Verses / Title / Topic:
Date:
Other:

Verses / Title / Topic:
Date:
Other:

Verses / Title / Topic:
Date:
Other:

Verses / Title / Topic:
Date:
Other:

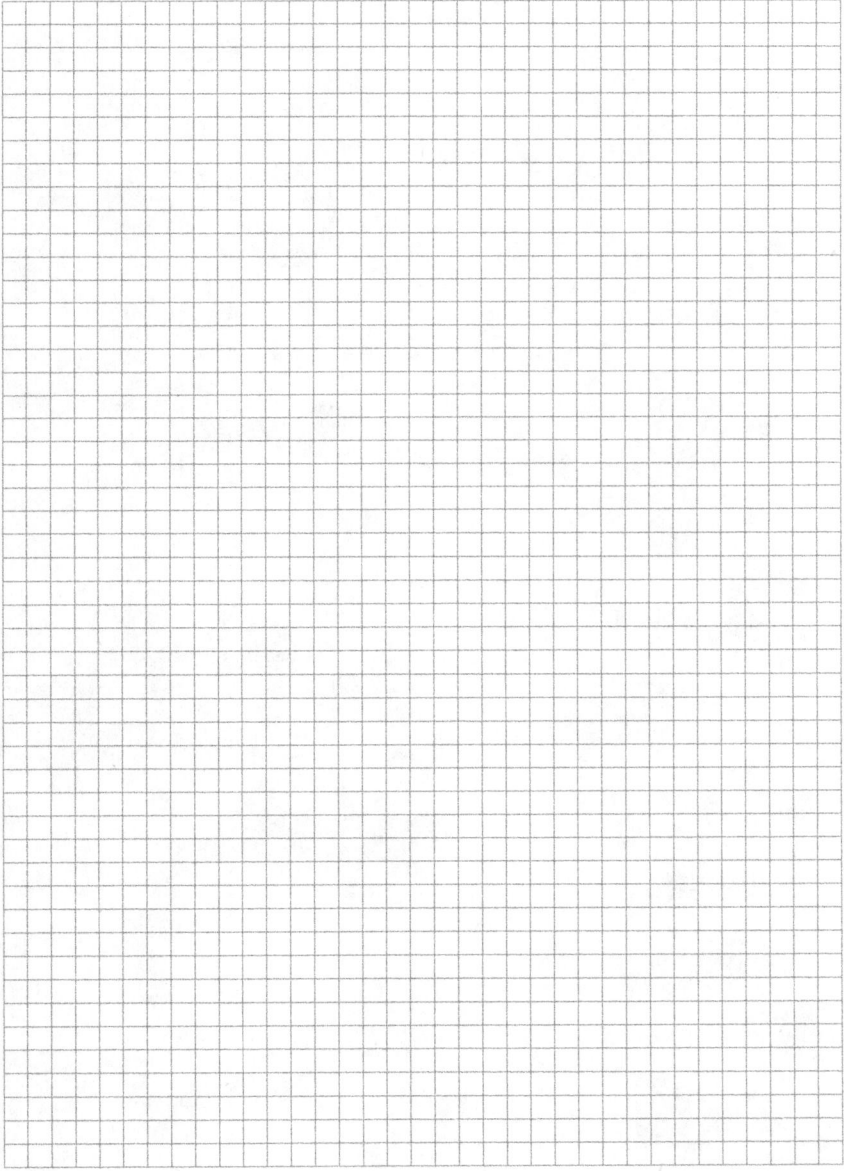

Verses / Title / Topic:
Date:
Other:

Verses / Title / Topic:
Date:
Other:

Verses / Title / Topic:
Date:
Other:

26

Verses / Title / Topic:
Date:
Other:

Verses / Title / Topic:
Date:
Other:

Verses / Title / Topic:
Date:
Other:

Verses / Title / Topic:
Date:
Other:

Verses / Title / Topic:
Date:
Other:

Verses / Title / Topic:
Date:
Other:

Verses / Title / Topic:
Date:
Other:

Verses / Title / Topic:
Date:
Other:

Verses / Title / Topic:
Date:
Other:

Verses / Title / Topic:
Date:
Other:

Verses / Title / Topic:
Date:
Other:

Verses / Title / Topic:
Date:
Other:

Verses / Title / Topic:
Date:
Other:

Verses / Title / Topic:
Date:
Other:

Verses / Title / Topic:
Date:
Other:

Verses / Title / Topic:
Date:
Other:

Verses / Title / Topic:
Date:
Other:

Verses / Title / Topic:
Date:
Other:

Verses / Title / Topic:
Date:
Other:

Verses / Title / Topic:
Date:
Other:

46

Verses / Title / Topic:
Date:
Other:

Verses / Title / Topic:
Date:
Other:

Verses / Title / Topic:
Date:
Other:

Verses / Title / Topic:
Date:
Other:

Verses / Title / Topic:
Date:
Other:

Verses / Title / Topic:
Date:
Other:

Verses / Title / Topic:
Date:
Other:

Verses / Title / Topic:
Date:
Other:

Verses / Title / Topic:
Date:
Other:

Verses / Title / Topic:
Date:
Other:

56

Verses / Title / Topic:
Date:
Other:

Verses / Title / Topic:
Date:
Other:

Verses / Title / Topic:
Date:
Other:

Verses / Title / Topic:
Date:
Other:

Verses / Title / Topic:
Date:
Other:

Verses / Title / Topic:
Date:
Other:

Verses / Title / Topic:
Date:
Other:

Verses / Title / Topic:
Date:
Other:

64

Verses / Title / Topic:
Date:
Other:

Verses / Title / Topic:
Date:
Other:

Verses / Title / Topic:
Date:
Other:

Verses / Title / Topic:
Date:
Other:

Verses / Title / Topic:
Date:
Other:

Verses / Title / Topic:
Date:
Other:

Verses / Title / Topic:
Date:
Other:

Verses / Title / Topic:
Date:
Other:

Verses / Title / Topic:
Date:
Other:

Verses / Title / Topic:
Date:
Other:

Verses / Title / Topic:
Date:
Other:

Verses / Title / Topic:
Date:
Other:

Verses / Title / Topic:
Date:
Other:

Verses / Title / Topic:
Date:
Other:

Verses / Title / Topic:
Date:
Other:

Verses / Title / Topic:
Date:
Other:

Verses / Title / Topic:
Date:
Other:

Verses / Title / Topic:
Date:
Other:

Verses / Title / Topic:
Date:
Other:

Verses / Title / Topic:
Date:
Other:

Verses / Title / Topic:
Date:
Other:

Verses / Title / Topic:
Date:
Other:

Verses / Title / Topic:
Date:
Other:

Verses / Title / Topic:
Date:
Other:

Verses / Title / Topic:
Date:
Other:

89

Verses / Title / Topic:
Date:
Other:

Verses / Title / Topic:
Date:
Other:

Verses / Title / Topic:
Date:
Other:

Verses / Title / Topic:
Date:
Other:

Verses / Title / Topic:
Date:
Other:

Verses / Title / Topic:
Date:
Other:

Verses / Title / Topic:
Date:
Other:

Verses / Title / Topic:
Date:
Other:

Verses / Title / Topic:
Date:
Other:

Verses / Title / Topic:
Date:
Other:

Verses / Title / Topic:
Date:
Other:

Verses / Title / Topic:
Date:
Other:

Verses / Title / Topic:
Date:
Other:

Verses / Title / Topic:
Date:
Other:

Verses / Title / Topic:
Date:
Other:

Verses / Title / Topic:
Date:
Other:

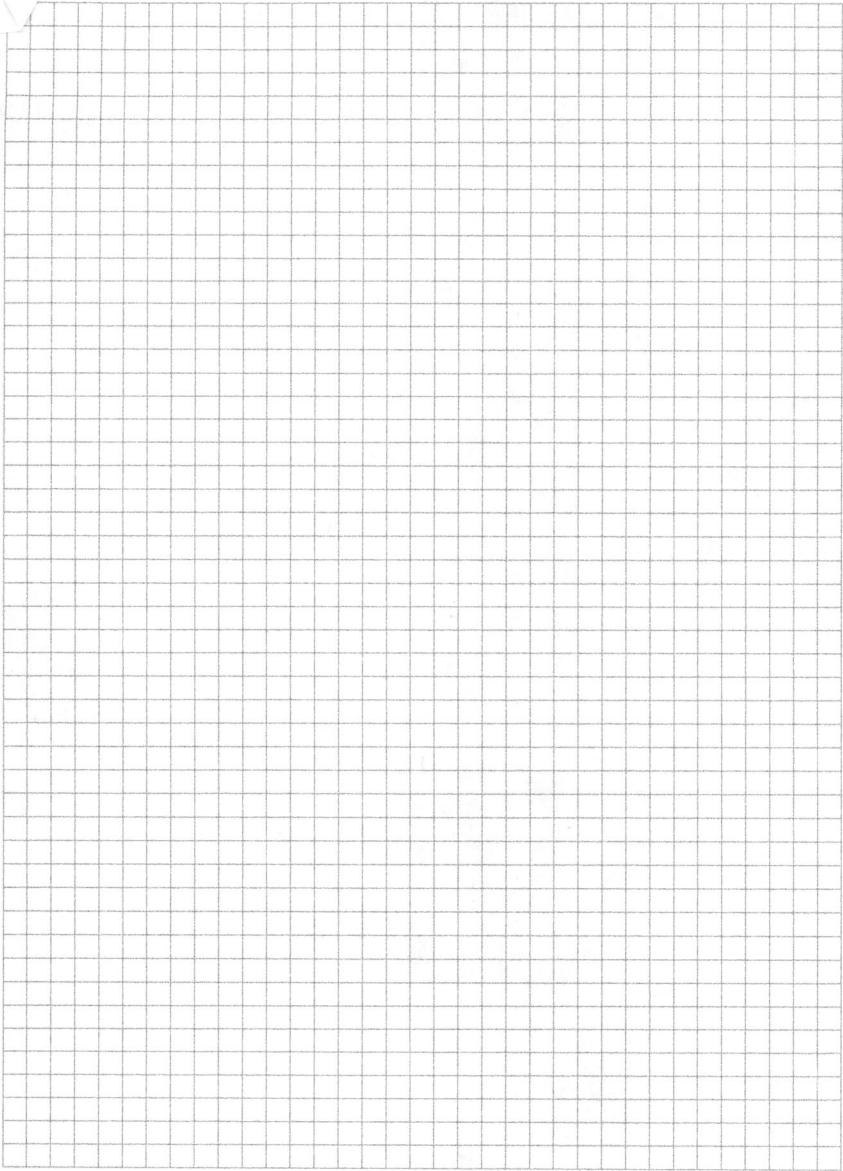

Title / Topic:

er:

Verses / Title / Topic:
Date:
Other:

Verses / Title / Topic:
Date:
Other:

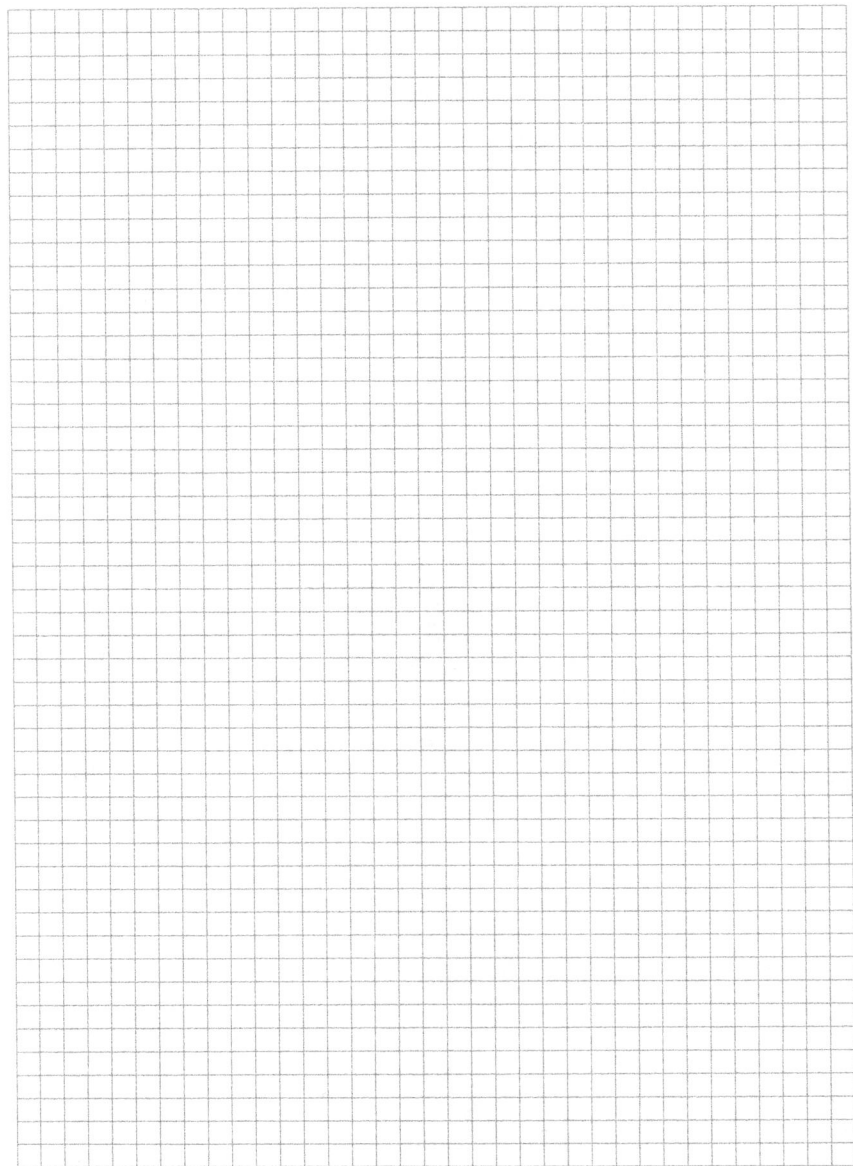

Verses / Title / Topic:
Date:
Other:

Verses / Title / Topic:
Date:
Other:

Verses / Title / Topic:
Date:
Other:

Verses / Title / Topic:
Date:
Other:

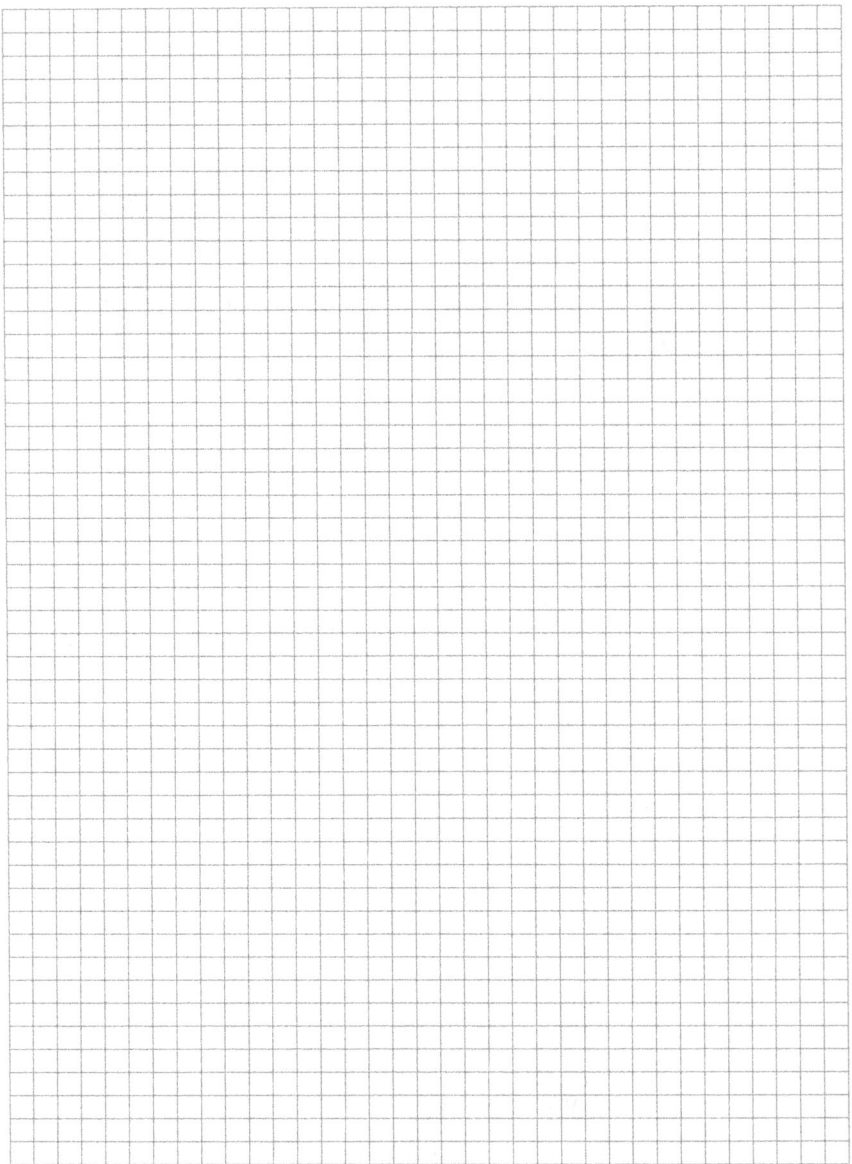

Verses / Title / Topic:
Date:
Other:

Verses / Title / Topic:
Date:
Other:

Verses / Title / Topic:
Date:
Other:

Verses / Title / Topic:
Date:
Other:

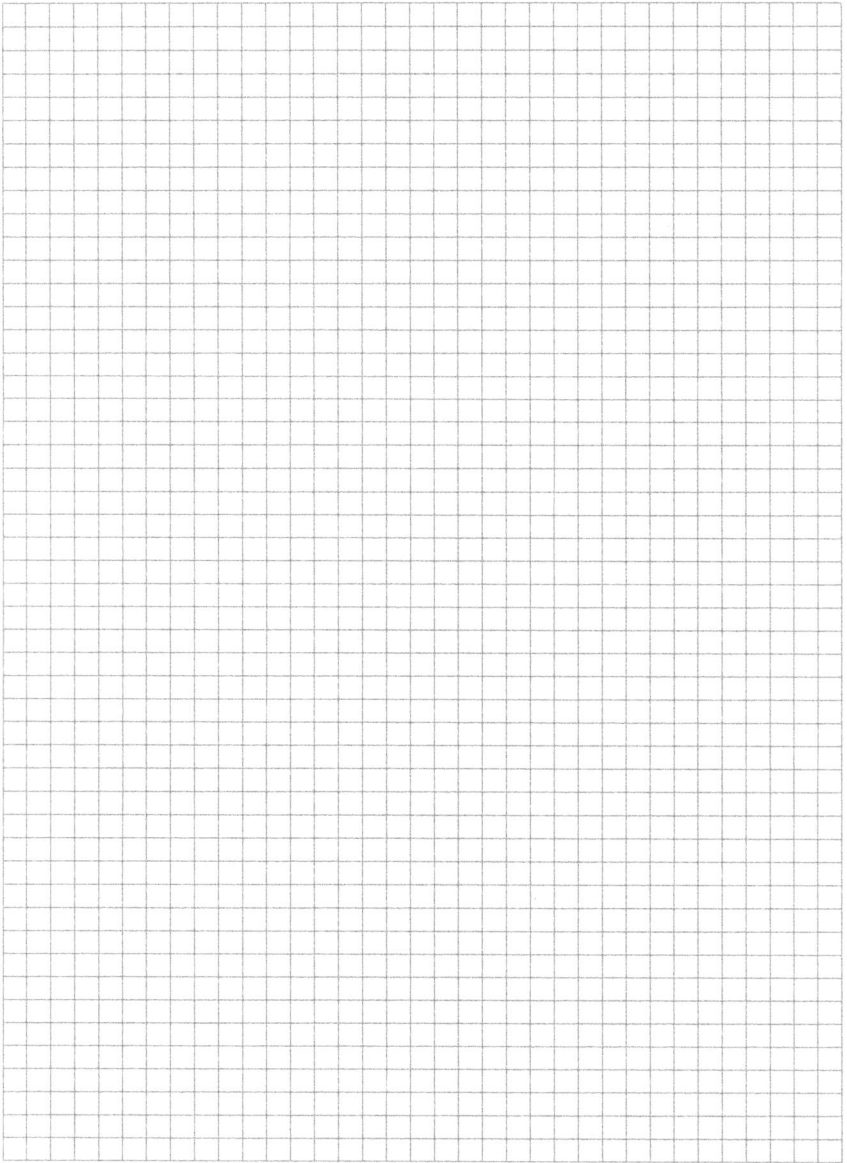

Verses / Title / Topic:
Date:
Other:

Verses / Title / Topic:
Date:
Other:

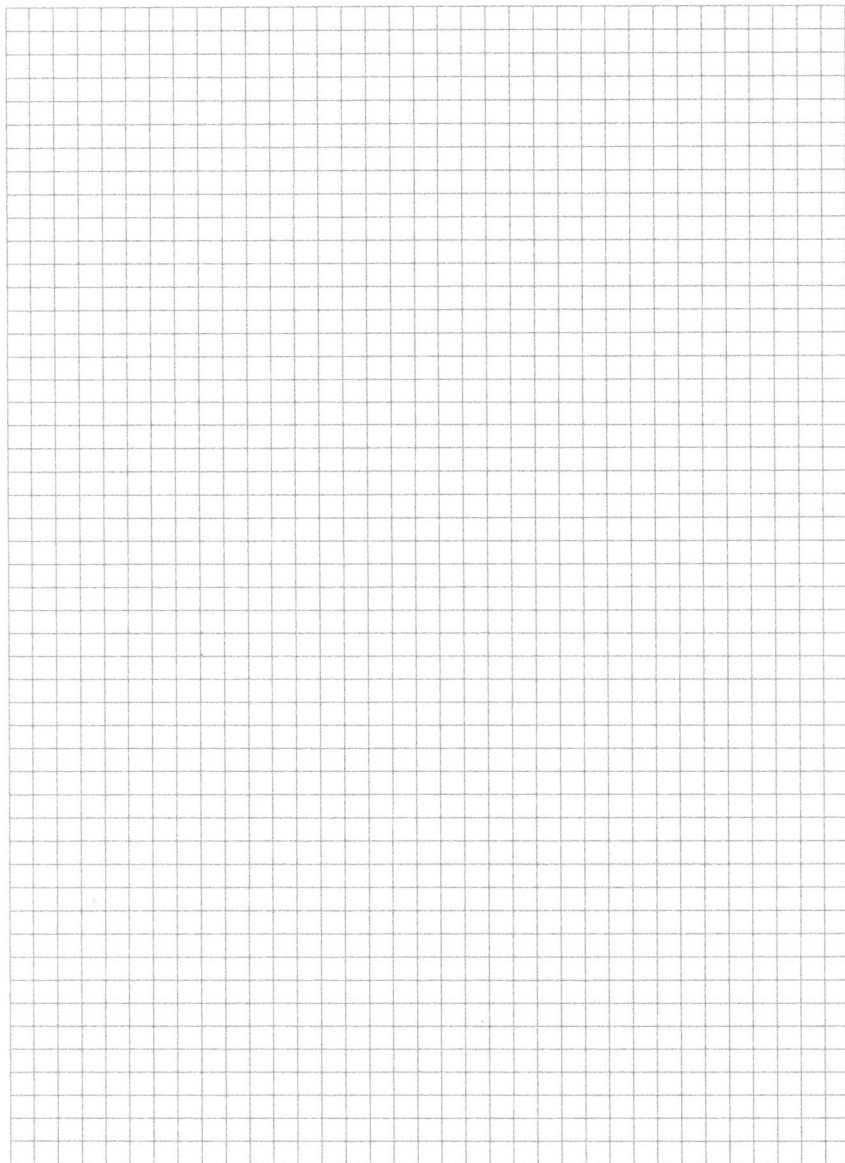

Verses / Title / Topic:
Date:
Other:

Verses / Title / Topic:
Date:
Other:

Verses / Title / Topic:
Date:
Other:

Verses / Title / Topic:
Date:
Other:

Verses / Title / Topic:
Date:
Other:

Verses / Title / Topic:
Date:
Other:

Verses / Title / Topic:
Date:
Other:

Verses / Title / Topic:
Date:
Other:

Verses / Title / Topic:
Date:
Other:

Verses / Title / Topic:
Date:
Other:

Verses / Title / Topic:
Date:
Other:

Verses / Title / Topic:
Date:
Other:

Verses / Title / Topic:
Date:
Other:

Verses / Title / Topic:
Date:
Other:

Verses / Title / Topic:
Date:
Other:

Verses / Title / Topic:
Date:
Other:

Verses / Title / Topic:
Date:
Other:

Verses / Title / Topic:
Date:
Other:

Verses / Title / Topic:
Date:
Other:

Verses / Title / Topic:
Date:
Other:

Verses / Title / Topic:
Date:
Other:

Verses / Title / Topic:
Date:
Other:

Verses / Title / Topic:
Date:
Other:

Verses / Title / Topic:
Date:
Other:

Verses / Title / Topic:
Date:
Other:

Verses / Title / Topic:
Date:
Other:

Verses / Title / Topic:
Date:
Other:

Verses / Title / Topic:
Date:
Other:

Verses / Title / Topic:
Date:
Other:

Verses / Title / Topic:
Date:
Other:

148

Verses / Title / Topic:
Date:
Other:

Verses / Title / Topic:
Date:
Other:

Verses / Title / Topic:
Date:
Other:

Verses / Title / Topic:
Date:
Other:

Verses / Title / Topic:
Date:
Other:

Verses / Title / Topic:
Date:
Other:

Verses / Title / Topic:
Date:
Other:

Verses / Title / Topic:
Date:
Other:

Verses / Title / Topic:
Date:
Other:

Verses / Title / Topic:
Date:
Other:

Verses / Title / Topic:
Date:
Other:

Verses / Title / Topic:
Date:
Other:

Verses / Title / Topic:
Date:
Other:

Verses / Title / Topic:
Date:
Other:

Verses / Title / Topic:
Date:
Other:

Verses / Title / Topic:
Date:
Other:

164

Verses / Title / Topic:
Date:
Other:

Verses / Title / Topic:
Date:
Other:

166

You've filled up every page (or skipped to the end)! If you enjoyed this, I hope you'll take a moment to check out my previous book:

THE REAL
Martin Luther

Read the first chapter free at therealmartinluther.com or from TheMinistryofWar.com.

As of this writing, about 2.2 billion people call themselves Christians. You would have a hard time finding something all of them agree on. Those differences can affect how we perceive our heroes of faith. We tend to only learn a small sliver about our heroes of faith. The good sliver.

The Real Martin Luther takes an honest look at this controversial historical figure. He's far more than the man behind the 95 Theses. With the help of more than 150 images, you can expect to smile, laugh and smirk while enjoying history that isn't dry or unnecessarily serious.

Did I mention you can get the first chapter free at therealmartinluther.com or theministryofwar.com?

I truly hope this book was helpful to you and your family.

What else would help?

How could this be improved?

Share your thoughts! Learn about our other projects at:

theMinistryofWar.com

www.ingramcontent.com/pod-product-compliance
Lightning Source LLC
Chambersburg PA
CBHW071855020426
42331CB00010B/2525